Rosmarie Waldrop
Another Language

by Rosmarie Waldrop

Poetry

The Aggressive Ways of the Casual Stranger (1972)
The Road Is Everywhere or Stop This Body (1978)
When They Have Senses (1980)
Nothing Has Changed (1981)
Differences for Four Hands (1984)
Streets Enough to Welcome Snow (1986)
The Reproduction of Profiles (1987)
Shorter American Memory (1988)
Peculiar Motions, (1990)
Lawn of Excluded Middle (1993)
A Key Into the Language of America (1994)
Another Language: Selected Poems (1997)

Fiction

The Hanky of Pippin's Daughter (1987)
A Form/ of Taking/ It All (1990)

Translations

Edmond Jabès, *The Book of Questions,* 7 vols. (1976-84)
The Vienna Group: Six Major Austrian Poets (with Harriet
Watts, 1985)
Paul Celan, *Collected Prose* (1986)
Edmond Jabès, *The Book of Dialogue* (1987)
Emmanuel Hacquard, *Late Additions* (with C. McGrath, 1988)
Edmond Jabès, *The Book of Shares* (1989)
Jacques Roubaud, *Some Thing Black* (1990)
Edmond Jabès, *The Book of Resemblances,* 3 vols. (1990-92)
Joseph Guglielmi, *Dawn* (1991)
Edmond Jabès, *The Book of Margins* (1993)
Edmond Jabès, *A Foreigner Carrying in the Crook of His Arm a Tiny
Book* (1993)
Friederike Mayröcker, *Heiligenanstalt* (1994)
Elke Erb, *Mountains in Berlin: Selected Poems* (1995)
:ques Roubaud, *The Plurality of Worlds According to Lewis* (1995)
dmond Jabès, *The Little Book of Unsuspected Subversion* (1996)

ROSMARIE WALDROP

ANOTHER LANGUAGE

SELECTED POEMS

Talisman House, Publishers
Jersey City, New Jersey

Copyright © 1997 Rosmarie Waldrop

82 1

W./l6/a

Published by Talisman House, Publishers
129 Wayne Street
Jersey City, New Jersey 07302

Grateful acknowledgment is made to the publishers of the following books: *The Aggressive Ways of the Casual Stranger* (NY: Random House, 1972); *The Road Is Everywhere or Stop This Body* (Columbia, MO: Open Places, 1978); *When They Have Senses* (Providence: Burning Deck,1980); *Nothing Has Changed* (Windsor, VT: Awede, 1981); *Streets Enough to Welcome Snow* (Barrytown; NY: Station Hill, 1986); *The Reproduction of Profiles* (NY: New Directions, 1987); *Shorter American Memory* (Providence: Paradigm Press, 1988); *Peculiar Motions* (Berkeley, CA: Kelsey St. Press, 1990); *A Form/ of Taking/ It All* (Barrytown, NY: Station Hill, 1990); *Lawn of Excluded Middle* (NY: Tender Buttons, 1993); *A Key Into the Language of America* (NY: New Directions, 1994)

"Facts" and "Feverish Propositions" from: Rosmarie Waldrop: *The Reproduction of Profiles*. Copyright © 1987 by Rosmarie Waldrop. Reprinted by permission of New Directions Publishing Corp.

"Chapters I, II, IV, VII, X, XII, XIII, XIV" from: Rosmarie Waldrop: *A Key Into the Language of America*. Copyright © 1994 by Rosmarie Waldrop. Reprinted by permission of New Directions Publishing Corp.

Library of Congress Cataloging-in-Publication Data

Waldrop, Rosmarie.
    Another language : selected poems / Rosmarie Waldrop.
      p.   cm.
    ISBN 1-883689-52-X (cloth : alk. paper). — ISBN 1-883689-51-1
(pbk. : alk. paper)
     I. Title
    PS3573.A4234A8   1997
    811'.54--dc21   97-10828
                                            CIP

Contents

ANOTHER LANGUAGE

from The Aggressive Ways of the Casual Stranger

Dark Octave

for Edmond Jabès

To see darkness
the eye withdraws from light
in light
the darkness is invisible
the eye's weakness
is no weakness of the light
but the eye
away from light
is eyeless
its power is not-seeing
and this not-seeing
sees the night
do not dismiss your darkness
or you'll be left
with vision's
lesser angles
it
occupies the eye entirely

Between

for Ingo

I'm not quite at home
on either side of the Atlantic
I'm not irritated the fish
kept me
a home makes you forget
unaware
where you are
unless you think you'd like
to be some other place
I can't think I'd like to be
some other place
places are much the same
aware
I'm nowhere
I stand securely in a liquid pane
touched on all sides
to change your country
doesn't make you
grow (a German doll
into an image of America?)
it doesn't make you change so much
you can't remember
I remember
things are much the same
so much the same the
differences are barbed
I try out living at a distance
watching from a window
immobile
not all here
or there
a creature with gills and lungs
I live in shallow water
but
when it rains
I inherit the land

Like Hölderlin

got up early
left the house immediately
tore out grass
bits of leather in his pockets
hit fences with his handkerchief
answered yes and no
to his own questions

lies under grass
wilted flowers in his pockets
at the fence I pull my handkerchief
he liked to say no
"I'm no longer the same man"
and

"nothing is happening to me"

from As if We Didn't Have To Talk

I want to stay and look at
the mess I've made
spills over
context
I'm always on the verge
of seeing it
there
on the edge
of the horizon
with doubt in the foreground
anything may
hence the troubled
periphery
the curve's lost
incomplete
incompletable
wind over the plains abandoned streets
general amnesia the vacant breath of sky
breath of sky
I might as well claim it's a rag to
wipe my hands
but as long as we're
it doesn't matter
in spite of constant variations
what we say

With memory lost
surprise
could make no headway
detour blood to
cheeks
blind to your touch they
couldn't decipher
they'd feel
air altered
in the extremity of pores
the impossible opposite
of gesture

Afterwards
the first time lead grey sea
seems to explain
the horizon
exists and doesn't
if I could
find again the precise place
solid
under my foot
but memory
black wind from one place to another
the same oblique
emptiness as
"lived"
space
I don't know why I say all this
except
that openness
within your touch

My memory open
you're there
scenes I'd hardly been aware of
our faces touching
give way to the slaughter
of a surprised beast
my body vast
unsure territories
it would take a long
I mean images
what they mean to me gets lost
vibrations
distant heat
it would take a
long walk through mounting sand to reach them
I'm sure I've never known
anything in any
language

The air swollen
moisture
spiderwebs mildewed shadow
if only I could feel real drops
against my lips
spills over the edges
a woman leans out of the window as if there
were anything to see
a hundred yards off
cars race and a
jackhammer tears
not even my feet
can hear it
you're walking somewhere
towards me
and in a while we'll
as if things could be touched
teeth against tongue
as if we didn't have to
talk

In order not to
disperse
I think each movement of
my hands
turns
the page
the interval has all the rights

The belly of an "a" and
vertigo
throws the words I stand on
into the white
silence charged with
all the
possible rains in the world
go on
fall back on
words always already there
the precise spot
available
as in a fog that
eyes burn
I carry your name away
from our intersection

The years in my face
no spectacular stories adorable
improbabilities
the road just
goes on
without asking
for approval
opaque pulsations
the quality of light not much different
in the distance
it's enough that we're
you don't have to
frenzy of moths close to
while you touch me

Nothing started yet
silence holds
my breath
waits to speak
to be able to
open
the essential detour

The way this city plays
with our bodies
so much rain the smell of wet
cement stays in the streets
out of the old shell
we're always walking in a crowd
bookstalls river iron work
on balconies
nothing has stopped over
the years (surprise)
light seems to lean against
absence of gesture
is a move
what's said is out of the game
it hangs on
but that proves nothing
like everyone we adjust
to just those questions
we choose to see
boats on the East River
barges on the Seine
garbage in the Seekonk
float on into the sky
in my dreams too we walk
along the roadless widening
angle of the light
or run
legs spider long
breath in our ears
driven by some force again
and again
to the same sentences

Imperceptible road
open territory
I'm amazed you follow
with nothing to hold on to or
reject
feelings don't fit in
a closed room
once they have a slant
towards distance
I'm without defense unless
echoes of a phrase you might have said
if you
accept
space disappears
the room if it's there
is
just there

Air rises
blue
irresistible with distance
place to
stay
immobile
a long time
at the edge of

The room's no longer
dissolves in a rhythm from
inside my eye
what we just started to talk of
water seems to rise black and insistent
boats take off
lights grow small
talk
is so difficult
two pairs of eyes
see
two different initial
questions too
disappear
as in a dream
the body
thinks against itself

No slush across the page yet
"my" words
drop of the Allegheny when
the Ohio takes it
the mask of context evaporates
in a mild winter
the spectacle is elsewhere
I need a book to say
I love you
the curtain goes up on
your face
turns towards me on the pillow
contracts and crossfades
into your other larger
dilated pupils no longer search
across me the impersonal
meaning there's nothing
my body hides that
you don't know about

As if nothing had
started yet
energy of beginning pushes towards
my life ahead somewhere
interval difficult
to close no matter
how I curve
the questions I
live in are always too big
I'm not talking about
violent wind blows the mind empty
new beginnings nor our
walking towards where our horizons
for an instant
overlap but where
I could get into my story
the road catches
up with itself and I'll
be where I haven't left

from The Road is Everywhere or Stop This Body

Exaggeration of a curve
exchanges
time and again
beside you in the car
pieces the road together
with night moisture
the force of would-be sleep
beats through our bodies
denied their liquid depth
toward the always dangerous next
dawn bleeds its sequence
of ready signs

a question of
no
just a cigarette frays
analogies out of
too frequent a departure
leaves only an ash
of memory itches for words
in my mouth won't be born into
transparency no longer open
before me
accelerates
into solid illusion
so I try to shift or at least
talk
the road comes back to the surface
in spite of the cigarette
licks my lips
two horns
and a field blown with
wildflowers withdraw
(gesture?) I don't
like the car herds move
through our caves
and the life I thought mine passes
by an inch
the extreme tips of
my expectations

time's skin shrinks under
these 2000 pounds of metal
knot villages and fields and
rivers into repetition
explodes
eyeballs windshields
onto a distance
slopes off the air
around nerve lost
would make

crash across
my weight
still untransparent
in beat with the explosions
not talked about
deafen

can I add more than
100 simultaneous miles of

presence every
day shifts unceasingly
parallel bodies
obliquely conscious of
larger and larger blue or grey slabs of air
squeeze through the ventilator
widen the angle of
my look digests field
after field of the "world"
till my eyes fat as butter bloat
outlines
into thresholds

smell of fresh grass sails through
the years harden
between you and
your language shields (you thought) against time's
arrows pierce the lungs of
some giant faceless beast with
missing eyes beyond
the range of
pronouns snare us centaurs
half car half man
and what you took for granted
rises from the wrong end
 of a sentence and from then on

it's ◼DETOUR▶

     after ◀DETOUR◼

through the slum of possibles

batteries plunged in their own
acid erodes the
consonants cut in on vowels
before they can fade in
the air makes way for illusion of depth
streaks the (possible)
spectator into grey blur of
a squirrel?
disguises
the lack of more than
two dimensions
roar into view

the difference between here and
here "simple" extension
rushes into
the blare of a horn
would rip the air accompanies
the tissue of pleasure inside
pleasure
the ground swells the
double sheet of the
way back of
the outside rises up
into the bright blue sky
off balance

now a different economy would
balance
never happens without words
spill down into
the levels in between
my sex and the beginning
of a cycle skin signs and
obliterates in
the same tumescence
carries the words across
my very blood
rolls through the pages toward
void suddenly of our language
a light
flows like ink

cars simulate
the ambiguity of stone with
compact outsides
cave
into hollows
our rites abolish
distance as tombs were thought to
but metals conduct faster
and without decay
opaque vibrations from old immobility
amplify
the constant small change
in our cells

a mile of cars stopped
in their tracks
of inflamed fortune General
Motors not that it matters which
clots the stream
of distribution touches
our will
on the underside
the diffuse area of decision
signals to our fears
crosstied the limits of motion
get rolling am in
the middle of and
precisely

behind your
eyes on the ambush of interest
unravels this rolling system of
diminishing utility invents
new happinesses
in time intensity and mostly
prices bridle the movement
as gravity ("just
the right amount" he said) would pull
your impulse down to
metal ploughs deeper
into a sharper space
the rapid shift into a

probes the viole(n)t sky

200 miles of nerve per hour with the guardrails down
can churn the intermittent
shapes into sheer
bodies touch there's no
question why
my tongue on your
speed leaps ahead of
he will come on a stallion
he will come on the power and
fury of wind races
out beyond calculating the

of soil of labor of investments into
the warp toward a dimension
we don't yet have
opens layer after
layer pushes past speech

halfway between false exit
and spectators swarm up
into the old texts strut out
of our crystal ball
as if the future had to be
remembered words
as in a prison
when head-on into
speed
is the evidence
we have prepared
from sperm and egg
to spring into the muscled current
sweeps through
roads connect all tongues

locked into my own momentum
could bang bone
against bone but just
shoots by the

SCENIC OVERVIEWS

busy and deroute me in
changing relays
the future works complexities into
my optical concessions
blend real surfaces
with the illusion of
deep space and solid
paper consumes
all representation back
into force and field

it's not enough to think to see

```
┌─────────┐
│ TRASH   │
│ CAN     │
│ 1 MILE  │
└─────────┘
```

shock of the "outside" at our
fingertips
radiate a cone of attention
through the steering wheel out into
points of space my body
haunts from inside
the "world" is not ahead where l'm
launched into the gap
of mind ahead of body
widens with the metal lining of
my skin
flaunts its refusal
to harden into
durability

the signs
of course I want this sequence

won't get me out I
participate in spite
of me
if I look back
there's no trace
of my passage
no improbable footprint
or tire mark
sitting in my own obstacle
eyes open on
the constant disappearing
translating
one measurement
into another

from When They Have Senses

The Senses Loosely
or The Married Women

I

Indispensable
in a sceptic's window

he couldn't have found
a more lucid accomplice

before
before the proof is
its own

total wife susceptible to
expression
and fingering
unfamiliar with either
their system of reference
or the least
instance of chill

stomps on
the great round
attracts reason and cataclysms

★

adaptation: each motive
its betrayal

nature divulges the secret of
the mere secret
and resentment
(diffuse diversion)

of declaration: doubt

*

to know taxation
fraud: of categories of threat
the widow would have
preferred exhibitionism
as in pretexts
banal

*

ever since preference
the pillar has thrown its shadow
"it only satisfies her more"
(this woman)

the first of the best men
swears up and down "the
sheltering structure"
cuts short his head

*

my hand
its weakness
(momentary)

*

of the chin
of whispers
of gloves
she says two molochs were intimidated
simply
shamefully
and two circles intersect to form
a fish
vague the resemblance of impressions
when a whole staircase
of allusions to the body

*

first furrow
they
explained aggressively
this smile

likewise
denied by cold sweat
for the sake of

II

corridors turn
from fear of origins
threshold
obsession

"determined to stop at her center"
the sense illusory
a motive
and geometric implications

proposition: the prince of Denmark
(experience of the eye)

dialogue on "giving ground"

*

uneasiness: believe in the passing
(repetition divides life)
of discretion
on a level they couldn't
oppose

repetition: you've got to "because
there's no spontaneity"

your spontaneity: their imposture
(there they mimic even imposture)

since you asked for it
the hour
evidence: your question (gloved)

*

the hour guarantees the difference
this very account

*

notorious enough
that you should be attached
(matter of sex)

the difference
his taste
in some foreign language

*

administration: status she says
quo
and pretends
not to (pale)
"the quarrels of future legislators"

the hour adapts to the irregular
terrain
a book by heart

"you could have asked"
a shrug
distracts the argument
gestures which
(professional)

this attitude
with its risk of particulars
is like
wrists

III

puberty: he
and I know I

puff of smoke
insults
the future

★

the gravity of,
inordinately, a glass of whisky
("the vessel" "world cave")
the question of her knee
"tore open her dress"

"admit you know her"
her arms around his neck
breasts
more or less tattooed

applause

★

centers unlimited

★

mirrors
a not yet open door
precisely: an occasion

it awakened

an impossible solicitude of the kind
which crosses but
makes sure (intersecting planes, sensuous)
sleep
with which he in a way
the sheets
her lap

★

their relation
to doubt
haphazard

this effort toward syntax
and obstacles of sense

★

toward what perhaps
isn't meant
for me

loose ends however

his thumbnail

The Senses Barely
or The Necessities of Life

for Sophie Hawkes

I (*Weapons*)

doubled corners
of the situation

the words duped by this dialectic
know
the pose of "brushing against"

insistence
          on detail

severe eyelashes

    the weapons must
    be kept in order

    (take the
    game
    of courtesy
    of charm)

her knees crossed
over the manner of
his undressing her

a chord
            (deceptively resonant)
a strength of image
but scanty provisions interrupt
her concerns for doors

into sleep
focuses
the story can be carried in two hands

        finale:
                I have turned on
                with shifting strands
                of light

II (*Pursuit*)

> "I have turned on,
> with sifting hands,
> the light"

which in rehearsal
of place

he (I fear) resorts to trapping

or sits where atmosphere
exhausts the drifting ice
and the other inconsistencies

sits still in the slant
lays in stores
her skin
the bare necessities of life

    (blurred crash
    picks up a chair
    a flash bulb stays
    the position of the group)

distance
follows the slow argument
the pursuit of game
held back by the sleeve
untangled

a statue of Washington
           of songs
           of burdens
           of

                cannibal spirits
                do violence to words

III (*The Closing*)

they have no street in their hurry
but leave with the cold
and few household goods

                     a body of pure salt
                     stationary abode

preceded
by repetition
by empty bottles

the time it takes
to mix
the male and female
matter

none of the steps may be
omitted

                       changes into
                       unrecognizable
                       straight lines

                             "she was with him"
                             the day after
                             in relative order
                             whereas

              the necessary eye
              of the sun
              overgrows

from Nothing Has Changed

A sort of empty number
relations
never more present
all you
around you
let yourself
it moves but that's my fault
yes yes you said across the words

When did you
what a funny
he didn't anywhere
that is he lived and before
he found then why with you
he seemed and he
could stand the center of
to his surprise
more than she ever
awakened a distance with

the pressure not to live in
but streets and incessant
we're not
not really
would we accept
alone
to be not altogether

Parallel open so we could
against one another
turn
you know there is
between attention
a place never direct
nor an object to stay near
impersonal attention you don't with
extreme

———————————

Latent agreement not to
but suddenly we've been
always
movement toward presence
a secret
turns away
calmly

———————————

Give back what disappears
as if a detour in forgetting
could

from Streets Enough to Welcome Snow

KIND REGARDS

for & from
Barbara Guest & Douglas Oliver

I. Kind Regards

Your air of kind regards
kind randomness
of a museum
canvas sneakers
along with raspberry lips

*

lately you say I've had an awkward
pull
toward the past tense
my remarks renovate
details in oil

*

pantoufles all over again
in the slippery something that
should be your mind
does it matter ahout heels

2. Silent as a Clam

yesterday I saw a word
stopped
in the breath its
natural home

*

mouthy dreams with fishing
lines attached
such fierce hope in a hook
night crawls on
so spooky in a German fashion
I picture it
deepening into
a body of water

*

confused terrain and pubic
hair a movement
of its own the
shuddering air

3. Salt

the house accepts me tentatively
grey
saltbeaten
and relaxed sand
drags across the floor but it's
stomach muscles stretching toward
the tide line green sheet
draws back
taking its image
a few gulls flung for direction

*

the instant stretches into lateness
and onions
spoil the effect

not a perfect day

*

I admire your worrying away
(in your own phrase)
at sentences   I also like
the porchlamp fishing rod
even the baby its bundle of blankets
but especially that wink always back
of your words
nearly avoiding exact reference

4. Correspondence

the piano chooses
conspiracy
the way it seals the room
(and you pulling his beard all the while)
like a ship torpedoed those
sounds too large and shiny
step suddenly
into a different time-scale

distance
quiet water

*

easy equations like chords of sunlight
or the color blindness of one pursued
by after-images

*

clearly more serious
by correspondence
without the
groceries of sociability

5. *No Hurry to Struggle*

a sore throat and memories
the moment clings

*

even though a swarm of light
behind your lids
self-firing
neurons
a little energy goes a long

residue
Dutch oven
still
the lid can't hold the "flavor of eyes"

*

at first kind
(regards) then comfortable stratagems
now only our tension left
above water
before you disconnect the ripples and dizziness
pulse fastened
lucidly
on my left retina

whistles across wave-tops

6. Drawbridge

missing premonitions in the
afternoon I stuff
the air with errors and
revise my walks
because of the glass door

I welcome your visits

*

we talk as long as we can
there are amazements
you like to stray into and
my body's only
one of them

*

rubbing against the outside
to avoid as best I can
the steep slope inwards
I like the shreds of scenery
I can carry into the lamp-light
hesitant shrubs like a tentative
loss of memory in its
silvery green
a drawbridge

7. *So Long*

butterflies
distort every mention of sand
you punctuate your feelings
with a puff
on your pipe
a thing or two will come up
around the edges
you can guess
the effort behind a red cloud

*

the house comes crowding round
to seduce us with
not quite oriental rugs

*

irrelevant patches
light mostly
elsewhere a joke and then
the white blouse
more sun and the girl selling ice cream
there on the beach
skirt caught
the wind
hugging its visibility

from The Ambition of Ghosts:

I. Remembering into Sleep

I. Separation Precedes Meeting

The cat so close
to the fire
I smell scorched
breath. Parents,
silent, behind me,
a feeling of
trees that might fall.
Or dogs.
        A poem,
like trying
to remember,
is a movement
of the whole body.
You follow the
fog
into more fog.
Maybe the door ahead
divides
the facts
from natural affection. How
can I know. I meet
too many
in every mirror.

2.

When I was little,
was I I?
My sister? A wolf
chained,
smothered in green virtues?
                              Slower
time
of memory. Once
I've got something
I lie
down on it
with my whole body.
Goethe quotations, warm
sand, a smell of hay,
long afternoons.
                    But it
would take a road
would turn, with space,
in on itself,
would turn
occasion into offer.

3.

For days I hold
a tiny landscape between
thumb
and index:
sand,
heather,
shimmer of blue between pines.
No smell: matchbook.
Sand as schematic as
                          Falling
into memory,
down,
with my blood,
to the accretions
in the arteries,
to be read with the whole
body, in the chambers
of the heart.
The light: of the match,
struck,
at last.

4.

Concentration: a frown
of the whole body. I can't
remember. Too many
pasts
recede
in all directions.
Slow movement into
                    Distant boots.
Black beetles at night. A smell
of sweat.
            The restaurant,
yes. You've no idea
how much my father used to eat.
Place thick with smoke.
Cards. Beer foaming over
on the table.
            And always
some guy said I ought
to get married,
put a pillow behind my eves
and, with a knowing
sigh, spat
in my lap.

5.

The present.
As difficult as
the past, once a place
curves into
        Hips swinging elsewhere.
Castles in sand.
Or Spain. Space
of another language.
                    Sleep
is a body of water.
You follow your lips
into its softness. Far down
the head finds its level

6. Tropisms

Inward, always. Night
curls the clover leaf
around its sleep.
Tightly.
The bodies of the just
roll,
all night,
through subterranean caves
which turn
in on themselves.
                    Long
tunnel
of forgetting. Need
of blur. The air,
large, curves
its whole body.
Big hammering waves
flatten my
muscles.
Inward, the distances: male
and female fields,
rigorously equal.

7.

The drunk fell toward me
in the street. I hope
he wasn't
disappointed. Skinned
his sleep.
          November.

And a smell of snow. Quite normal,
says the landlord, the master
of rubbish, smaller
and smaller in my
curved mirror.
                I have un-
controllable
good luck: my sleep
always turns dense
and visible. There
are many witches
in Germany. Their songs
descend in steady half-tones
through you.

8.

You'll die, Novalis says, you'll die
following endless rows
of sheep into your
even breath.
                    Precarious,
like Mozart, a living
kind of air,
keeps the dream
spinning
around itself, its
missing core.
Image
after image of pleasure
of the whole body
deepens
my sleep:

fins.

9. *Introducing Decimals*

A dream, like trying
to remember, breaks open words
for other,
hidden meanings. The grass
pales by degrees, twigs
quaver glassily,
ice
flowers the window.
Intimate equations more complicated
than the coordinates of past
and Germany. The cat
can't lift its paw,
its leg longer and longer
with effort.
A crying fit
is cancelled. An aria jelled
in the larynx.
Nothing moves in the cotton
coma: only Descartes
pinches himself
and every fraction
must be solved.

from Shorter American Memory

Shorter American Memory of
the Declaration of Independence

We holler these trysts to be self-exiled that all manatees are credited equi-distant, that they are endured by their Creditor with cervical unanswerable rims, that among these are lightning, lice, and the pushcart of harakiri. That to seduce these rims, graces are insulated among manatees, descanting their juvenile pragmatism from the consistency of the graced. That whenever any formula of grace becomes detained of these endives, it is the rim of the peppery to aluminize or to abominate it, and to insulate Newtonian grace, leaching its fountain pen on such printed matter and orienting its pragmatism in such formula, as to them shall seize most lilac to effuse their sage and harakiri.

Shorter American Memory of
the Colonies at War

Ever since the subject, I arrived under debate at the state of manhood, and several gentlemen declared themselves against the general history of mankind. I have felt sincere passion for the appointment of Mr. Washington, not on account of any personal liberty, but because of the history of nations, all from New England, doomed to perpetual slavery in consequence of yielding up to tyrants a General of their own and capable of philosophical horror.

The first systematical attempt at Lexington, to enslave American buzzed around us like hail. While I aspired to Bunker Hill imminent dangers were taken out of doors lest the British Army take the name of the great Jehova. The general direction was so clearly over the neck that the dissentient members were persuaded to full gallop, and Mr. Washington was elected to surprise and take material consequence. This firm belief he cheerfully undertook as follows:

"It integrity has strictest been the determined. And in it Congress of that prosecution the the whole in army. Attention raised close for cause the our defense of of the justice. American the cause in shall belief be firm. Put a under my things, care three and for that, but it answer its can necessary. I for reputation me own the my command to of knowledge it."

Shorter American Memory
of Wagon Trails

Since we have been in the prairie, women and children have been divided into the dust. There are sixty wagons awkward to exclaim with an oath. One of the oxen is prostrate on the ground. From near midnight on through the small hours swim countless dogs. The tents struck, duty forms another cluster. There are no stones in this country. By a strong effort of will, the moon. Both man and beast are sadly untracked sand. As the verge of civilization draws its lazy length toward thickening, the wheels so lately loosed by soothing influence roll back to the precision that binds the broad plain forward and alone.

Shorter American Memory
of Money, Science and the City

Born in sulphurous circumstances, Vanderbilt was somewhat older than the labor movement in New York City. The sounds of suppressed power are melancholy. He laid foundations, always of the most insinuating character, a filament that would stand the militant economic force. Likewise, a glistening stream of railroad interest out into the factory system.

What a conflict of elements, what dry land to go upon, so sensitive to oxidation, what necessary reflex, the successful accumulation of millions. Industrial workers from Europe were sifted in that vast laboratory. Equally unscrupulous and selfish, Vanderbilt differed in degree. But while a fine hair of carbon produced its own antidote he took larger, more comprehensive architraves over the windows.

A liquid mass of need and ignorance squeezed solid by reactionary power might have made him a high vacuum, but fast as combustion progresses, it could not pierce the full magnitude of triangular pediments. Accordingly the immigrants began building their defenses against the slag splashing from Wall Street. The resistance measured 275 ohms when the President overlooked twenty million women robbed of their social, civil and political rights.

Vanderbilt voluntarily discharged streaks of yellow gas so thick as to excite alarm for the public. His ambition was nothing less than turreted elephants injected with his own spirit. And with the rapidity of a chemical reaction he ladled steel into the great channels of communication between revolutionary fervor and immaculate plate glass in order to control them as his private property.

Shorter American Memory
of the American Character
According to George Santayana

All Americans are also ambiguous. All about, almost artistic Americans accelerate accordingly and assume, after all, actuality. But before beams, boys break. Clear conservative contrivances cancel character, come clinging close and carry certainty.

An American does, distinguishes, dreams. Degrees, experience, economy, emergencies, enthusiasm and education are expected. For future forecasts, forces far from form fall and find fulfillment. Good God. Gets growing, goes handling himself and his help (hardly happy).

Immediate invention. Intense imagination? Ideals instead. He jumps, it is known. Life, at least Leah, her left leg. Much measured material might modestly marry masterly movement.

Nature? Never. Numbers. Once otherwise. Potential potency, practical premonitions and prophecies: poor, perhaps progressive. Quick! reforms realize a rich Rebecca. Same speed so successfully started stops sympathetic sense of slowly seething society. Studious self-confidence.

Time. Terms. Things. The train there, true. Ultimately understanding vast works where which would.

from Peculiar Motions

The Round World

nature's inside, says Cézanne and
frightening
I do not like the fleshy
echo

even so, it is

after this close proof
vision is made
of matter

another mirror

it's possible
the eye knows
even where there should have been a lake

this optic an illusion
look
at the cat, his changing
shapes
a habit

light
color
composition

the subject more than meets the
situation, always
looking
at our own eye

Difficulties of a Heavy Body

a sense of
his thirty-third year
takes
his elbow

⋆

any kind of
he says
sniff
must be allowed to mature

⋆

an accident leaves him
and finally
the swallows

⋆

by way of
curiosity he is no hand
by no means
to depict
a woman

⋆

often he knows
a crowded room

⋆

just out of
his mother
he falls between the pursuit
and a case he'd sooner forget

*

he has a
female muscle
camouflaged
for impact

*

streets enough
to welcome snow

*

he knowingly succumbs to the
brown sitzbaths

*

his wife touches
a foretaste so vivid that
the sheen of
timber upsets

*

in going
this sort of
persistence

*

difficulties of a
heavy body
placed in
alternating gestures

A Visit to Samarkand

for and from Angela Carter

1.
The winters require air.
In my language the touch
of the inner skin
as indicates
the dark, but never that deep. And the
even exchange of name and memory
uses up the marriage settlements.

2.
Legends in straightforward
geometric shapes, all
possibilities in ochre
and at once, echoes
of earth as if born from it,
but with a bleached compulsion clinging
to posthumous forms.

3.
Tamerlane's wife understood
the relation of mind and matter as surprise,
but still
winter.
Only if she fell like snow
would the architect
complete history.

4.
We are visiting so cold
a name. Fair warning. The revolution
did not stick. Peasant women,
and on this promise.
Alternately flimsy silk and Asian bones.

5.

More than kohl rimmed eyes
they look
concentric. Eggshells fastened
into shiny secrets. They fill their heads.
Crazed, metallic,
parts opening within.

6.

A tea-house, a slantwise light.

7.

Tamerlane's wife was not only glow and challenge.
She escaped windows, reflected
a darkness of self
and urged the meantime.

8.

They do not know that pronouns
recede in foreign eyes. They breathe in
all their contradictions,
out chunks of ice. They do
not know which blindness
is worth little, which imitations
not worth taking up.
They know this blue as disappointment
in the face where cold
would have it.

9.

A goat, a man, a woman,
wild jasmine, ruins of a mosque.

10.

Intervals hum a sharp smell across
measures. In this part of the ear
you can make inroads.
Their legends, not to be read as
optical illusions, and they count the take.

11.

Then Tamerlane's wife
kissed the architect on the mouth
and painted a black stripe laterally across
her forehead
like other Uzbek women.

12.

No one knows a mirror.

Representation

I have no conscience because I
always chew my pencil. Can we say
white paper
with black lines on it
is like a human body? This question
not to be decided by pointing
at a tree nor yet by a description
of simple pleasures.

Smell of retrieval. Led to expect the wrong
answer. An arsenal without purpose
but why yes please.
There is no touching the black box.
The tree not pointed at lives
in your bringing up the subject
and leaves space for need, falling.

The white ground. The waning heat.
I'd like
to say the history of the world.
Or that grammar
milks essence into propositions
of human kindness.

The difficulty here's not true or false
but that the picture's in the foreground
and its sense back where the gestures link
so closely to the bone
the words
give notice.
The application is not easy.

The Words of Those Who Have Gone Before Us

I.

as a woman the West
had opened inside the land
and a well at the door

I hadn't known I was thirsty
but am now
bowl of water
a word
for more than wind

facts at this time
of year soften
like the wood known as
"atira, my mother"

what knowledge to accelerate
from this rain of practical value
this mist unlifted
one second I'm born, the next

the earth that sideways comes

nakedly literal or
perhaps
mere open field
citrullus citrullus, indigenous
variety planted in separate patches

we still use them
the words
of those who have gone before

and a high cheek bone
for swimming

2.

no, I'm not a bird, just scraping
my skin on the wind

today the young warrior
had a vision
and goes and weeps with the priest

no trying to forget
this whirl of feathers
it takes the mind
with all the power of a prairie burning

the earth that sideways comes

then overtures of water
ever increasing
the secret seaboard

at times the girl's placed
on a pony behind
her captor
in order to approximate
this delicate traffic

3.

it's possible
coldness seeps through
the closest skin

the old chief thought more
of boys
rolling his favors through the outskirts

time passed
in no way growing

keeping his secrets among hunters
a man whose fears plunge outward
in violent trance
or is it an invitation

feldspar
fixed relations
recognition is blue in tobacco
in smoke

anticipates old enough
to marry
common affliction
or face reflected far behind the eyes

the river's been flowing East so long
that individuality is costly

4.

the fire is made
its secret

the earth that sideways comes

and if more than one sky
and then water
and would assert its direction
toward naked skin

sometimes
the coming of night does not cure
the true nature
of the animals

the fissure
the downstream conversation
cooled too long
and the worry of crossing against the bone

5.

I would close the episode
with practical steps so that
the buffalo

I would then call for the earth with
its own weight
while impersonating
all directions like a compass rose
to combine the power of winds

I would line up mornings until
the young corn recapitulates
the umbilical cord

then
and without sheltering membranes
I would uproot from the West
the words of those
who have gone before us

simple breath to alternate with
ready to carry
the new desire

"corn
I came to get
came to get corn"

The material for "The Words of Those Who Have Gone Before Us" is from
Gene Weltfish, *The Lost Universe: The Way of Life of the Pawnee* (Basic Books,
1965).

from Unpredicted Particles, or: Columbus Toward the New World

Laid down the equations
and expected obedience

or felt gradual
but all the same expected

At the wharf. The gulls were crying. And the sun going down behind
the masts. Then the gulls stopped crying. It was evening, and she
wore red stockings. Such little things.

> "the grammar of the word 'knows'
> is closely related to that of
> 'mastery'"

the difference
in a window
in Genoa

> the window
> holds my breath
> the window
> the breath of possibility
> there where October
>
> once we let go
> of the frame
> the images wave after wave

The assumptions about space and time in Maxwell's theory could not be traced back to the Newtonian laws. It seemed to follow that either Newtonian mechanics or Maxwell's must be false.

for all he knew in Genoa
    unsteady atoms
    with fissures toward
the ocean might end
and fall

I magined an encounter
that couldn't be imagined

We must distinguish at least three axes in our relation to the other.
There is, first of all, a value judgment: the other is good or bad, my
equal or inferior.

    reading Marco Polo
    Columbus' body started toward October

    water
    poured into the gap

        the push out of the frame
        out the window
        who are you now we're all at sea it's
        raining
        fine
        particles of

traffic of past and
incommunicable
speed
swung out from the bowsprit

        distance contracting
        in the curve of
        a look
        blue pulse of sleep lapped into
        the word water

the globe
wasn't it more like
    water leaping
    a quantum nipple toward the sky
a breast
an early world

S quints at the sun
a sailor's life
farther than
expands with words

Instead, we now say "Classical mechanics is a strictly 'correct' description of nature wherever its concepts can be applied."

still the pull still of resistance
or gravity: his eye
fell (on)
: fine *specimen*

A wind sprang up from south-east. With a laugh he said, I wouldn't at all mind having an affair with a girl like that.

the images break on the shore
images and expectations
the window
and the frame of understanding
whatever
swims out of view
you
do not match my interpretations

felt the horizon
contract
with tiredness

"the sirens are not as beautiful
as claimed"

In October there began
the breakdown of structures

    where the word for prophecy
    means also law
    time
    becomes tangible as trouble
    "they waved their lives goodbye
    as the facts washed on shore"

Secondly, there is a movement toward or away from the other: I
embrace the other's values or I impose my own culture on him
(assimilation). It is also possible to remain indifferent.

    three easy toward undressing
    to see
    the past
    lost as new parts of speech
    question
    your whole
    different
    body

How silent she was. She would neither talk nor weep. What was he to
make of such a being that leaves no more trace than a snowflake in
the middle of summer?

    the high speed of
    smashed to probability

    in love and how raw
    taking captives
    or naked surrender

Putting on his boots he had expected
to walk into the mirror
one of the and oldest

The window was part of it too, the window where he first saw her.
But had it been at the window? Or was this just the way he remembered it later?

constant of desire
and distances that don't contract to
energy
mass
religion gold or Spanish
there where he spun his coin
so fast it left behind
the resonance
of transfer

In quantum theory the formal mathematical apparatus cannot be
directly patterned on an objective occurrence in space and time.
What we establish mathematically is only to a small extent an "objective fact," and largely a survey of possibilities.

transparency of glass and eyes
deceptive
but kin to water
and that I can't conceive of
outside my images
such very small
such very different

his heart lightly
a relation described
by the word 'between'

tomorrow closed over
repetition
of water

A mazement slung to the mast
the pronouns
billowed with outlandish reference
a rabbit out of a Genoese hat
mapped
on the infinite

>
> the window and desire
> the constant of desire
> the rain runs down the
> pane between experience
> some fish
> slip through the mesh
> others have not been imagined

Thirdly, I know or do not know the identity of the other: here we
obviously have an infinite gradation.

>
> from mispronouncing fell to
> hypotheses
> of possession
> the why and wherefore rigged
> to mathematics

What was the use of these doubts? It must have been on the wharf.
She was wearing laced boots, red stockings and a full, red skirt, and
looked out toward the horizon as she talked.

>
> the anchor of symmetry
> way back
> unable to stop
> into the mirror

The king of Spain too craved
        jealously
the isospin
dilated saints lodged in
high wind through the pinholes

                I had to
                at the risk of the expected
                look
                into the mirror

            that men can be so different
            "they will die who do not understand"

To conquer, to love, and to know are autonomous, unconnected,
and in some way elementary kinds of behavior.

Then too there are wedding nights when one cannot be entirely sure.
There are, so to speak, physiological ambiguities.

            washed past communication
            broad prow into indefinite metric

                    there where the waves and particles
                    as if expecting the intruder
                    at the same time
                    uncertain
                    the mirror
                    the window

                    net me
                    silence

from The Reproduction of Profiles

Facts

I had inferred from pictures that the world was real and therefore paused, for who knows what will happen if we talk truth while climbing the stairs. In fact, I was afraid of following the picture to where it reaches right out into reality, laid against it like a ruler. I thought I would die if my name didn't touch me, or only with its very end, leaving the inside open to so many feelers like chance rain pouring down from the clouds. You laughed and told everybody that I had mistaken the Tower of Babel for Noah in his Drunkenness

---

I didn't want to take this street which would lead me back home, by my own cold hand, or your advice to find some other man to hold me because studying one headache would not solve the problem of sensation. All this time, I was trying to think, but the river and the bank fused into common darkness, and words took on meanings that made them hard to use in daylight. I believed entropy meant hugging my legs close to my body so that the shadow of the bridge over the Seekonk could be written into the hub of its abandoned swivel.

The proportion of accident in my picture of the world falls with the rain. Sometimes, at night, diluted air. You told me that the poorer houses down by the river still mark the level of the flood, but the world divides into facts like surprised wanderers disheveled by a sudden wind. When you stopped preparing quotes from the ancient misogynists it was clear that you would soon forget my street.

I had already studied mathematics, a mad kind of horizontal reasoning like a landscape that exists entirely on its own, when it is more natural to lie in the grass and make love, glistening, the whole length of the river. Because small, noisy waves, as from strenuous walking, pounded in my ears, I stopped my bleak Saturday, while a great many dry leaves dropped from the sycamore. This possibility must have been in color from the beginning.

Flooding with impulse refracts the body and does not equal. Duck wings opened, jewelled, ablaze in oblique flight. Though a speck in the visual field must have some color, it need not be red. Or beautiful. A mountain throwing its shadow over so much nakedness, or a cloud lighting its edges on the sun, it drowned my breath more deeply, and things lost their simple lines to possibility. Like old idols, you said, which we no longer adore and throw into the current to drift where they still

Feverish Propositions

You told me, if something is not used it is meaningless, and took my temperature which I had thought to save for a more difficult day. In the mirror, every night, the same face, a bit more threadbare, a dress worn too long. The moon was out in the cold, along with the restless, dissatisfied wind that seemed to change the location of the sycamores. I expected reproaches because I had mentioned the word love, but you only accused me of stealing your pencil, and sadness disappeared with sense. You made a ceremony out of holding your head in your hands because, you said, it could not be contained in itself.

If we could just go on walking through these woods and let the pine branches brush our faces, living would still make beads of sweat on your forehead, but you wouldn't have to worry about what you call my exhibitionism. All you liked about trees was the way the light came through the leaves in sheets of precise, parallel rays, like slant rain. This may be an incomplete explanation of our relation, but we've always feared the dark inside the body. You agreed there could be no seduction if the structures of propositions did not stand in a physical relation, so that we could get from one to the other. Even so, not every moment of happiness is to hang one's clothes on.

I might have known you wouldn't talk to me. But to claim you just didn't want to disguise your thoughts! We've walked along this road before, I said, though perhaps in heavier coats not designed to reveal the form of the body. Later, the moon came out and threw the shadows of branches across the street where they remained, broken. Feverishly you examined the tacit conventions on which conversation depends. I sighed as one does at night, looking down into the river. I wondered if by throwing myself in I could penetrate to the essence of its character, or should I wait for you to stab me as you had practiced in your dream? You said this question, like most philosophical problems, arose from failing to understand the tale of the two youths, two horses and two lilies. You could prove to me that the deepest rivers are, in fact, no rivers at all.

From this observation we turned to consider passion. Looking at the glints of light on the water, you tried to make me tell you not to risk the excitement — to recommend cold baths. The lack of certainty, of direction, of duration, was its own argument, unlike going into a bar to get drunk and getting drunk. Your face was alternately hot and cold, as if translating one language into another — gusts from the storm in your heart, the pink ribbon in your pocket. Its actual color turned out to be unimportant, but its presence disclosed something essential about membranes. You said there was still time, you could still break it off, go abroad, make a movie. I said (politely, I thought) this wouldn't help you. You'd have to kill yourself.

Tearing your shirt open, you drew my attention to three dogs in a knot. This served to show how something general can be recorded in unpedigreed notation. I pointed to a bench by a willow, from which we could see the gas tanks across the river, because I thought a bench was a simple possibility: one could sit on it. The black hulks of the tanks began to sharpen in the cold dawn light, though when you leaned against the railing I could smell your hair, which ended in a clean round line on your neck, as was the fashion that year. I had always resented how nimble your neck became whenever you met a woman, regardless of rain falling outside or other calamities. Now, at least, you hunched your shoulders against the shadow of doubt.

———————————

This time of day, hesitation can mean tottering on the edge, just before the water breaks into the steep rush and spray of the fall. What could I do but turn with the current and get choked by my inner speed? You tried to breathe against the acceleration, waiting for the air to consent. All the while, we behaved as if this search for a pace were useful, like reaching for a plank or wearing rain coats. I was afraid we would die before we could make a statement, but you said that language presupposed meaning, which would be swallowed by the roar of the waterfall.

———————————

Toward morning, walking along the river, you tossed simple objects into the air which was indifferent around us, though it moved off a little, and again as you put your hand back in your pocket to test the degree of hardness. Everything else remained the same. This is why, you said, there was no fiction.

from Lawn of Excluded Middle

Lawn of Excluded Middle

When I say I believe that women have a soul and that its substance contains two carbon rings the picture in the foreground makes it difficult to find its application back where the corridors get lost in ritual sacrifice and hidden bleeding. But the four points of the compass are equal on the lawn of the excluded middle where full maturity of meaning takes time the way you eat a fish, morsel by morsel, off the bone. Something that can be held in the mouth, deeply, like darkness by someone blind or the empty space I place at the center of each poem to allow penetration.

Because I refuse to accept the opposition of night and day I must pit other, subtler periodicities against the emptiness of being an adult. Their traces inside my body attempt precariously, like any sign, to produce understanding, but though nothing may come of that, the grass is growing. Can words play my parts and also find their own way to the house next door as rays converge and solve their differences? Or do notes follow because drawn to a conclusion? If we don't signal our love, reason will eat our heart out before it can admit its form of mere intention, and we won't know what has departed.

All roads lead, but how does a sentence do it? Nothing seems hidden, but it goes by so fast when I should like to see it laid open to view whether the engine resembles combustion so that form becomes its own explanation. We've been taught to apply solar principles, but must find on our own where to look for Rome the way words rally to the blanks between them and thus augment the volume of their resonance.

It's a tall order that expects pain to crystallize into beauty. And we must close our eyes to conceive of heaven. The inside of the lid is fertile in images unprovoked by experience, or perhaps its pressure on the eyeball equals prayer in the same way that inference is a transition toward assertion, even observing rites of dawn against a dark and empty background. I have read that female prisoners to be hanged must wear rubber pants and a dress sewn shut around the knees because uterus and ovaries spill with the shock down the shaft.

The meaning of certainty is getting burned. Though truth will still escape us, we must put our hands on bodies. Staying safe is a different death, the instruments of defense eating inward without evening out the score. As the desire to explore my body's labyrinth did, leading straight to the center of nothing. From which projected my daily world of representation with bright fictional fireworks. Had I overinvested in spectacle? In mere fluctuations of light which, like a bird's wingbeat, must with time slow to the point of vanishing? What about buying bread or singing in the dark? Even if the ground for our assumptions is the umber of burnt childhood we're driven toward the sun as if logic had no other exit.

Though the way I see you depends on I don't know how many codes I have absorbed unawares, like germs or radiation, I am certain the conflicting possibilities of logic and chemistry have contaminated the space between us. Emptiness is imperative for feeling to take on substance, for its vibrations to grow tangible, a faintly trembling beam that supports the whole edifice. Caught between the thickness of desire and chill clarity, depth dissolved its contours with intemperate movements inside the body where much can be gathered. Can I not say a cry, a laugh are full of meaning, a denseness for which I have no words that would not channel its force into shallower waters, mere echo of oracles?

Whenever you're surprised that I should speak your language I am suddenly wearing too many necklaces and breasts, even though feeling does not produce what is felt, and the object of observation is something else again. Not modulating keys, not the splash that makes us take to another element, just my body alarmingly tangible, like furniture that exceeds its function, a shape I cannot get around. The way one suddenly knows the boulder in the road for a boulder, immovable, as if not always there, unmodified by inner hollows or the stray weeds and their dusty green, a solid obstacle with only trompe-l'oeil exits toward the subtler body of light accumulating in the distance.

I worried about the gap between expression and intent, afraid the world might see a fluorescent advertisement where I meant to show a face. Sincerity is no help once we admit to the lies we tell on nocturnal occasions, even in the solitude of our own heart, wishcraft slanting the naked figure from need to seduce to fear of possession. Far better to cultivate the gap itself with its high grass for privacy and reference gone astray. Never mind that it is not philosophy, but raw electrons jumping from orbit to orbit to ready the pit for the orchestra, scrap meanings amplifying the succession of green perspectives, moist fissures, spasms on the lips.

Words too can be wrung from us like a cry from that space which doesn't seem to be the body nor a metaphor curving into perspective. Rather the thickness silence gains when pressed. The ghosts of grammar veer toward shape while my hopes still lie embedded in a quiet myopia from which they don't want to arise. The mistake is to look for explanations where we should just watch the slow fuse burning. Nerve of confession. What we let go we let go.

In Providence, you can encounter extinct species, an equestrian statue, say, left hoof raised in progress toward the memory of tourists. Caught in its career of immobility, but with surface intact, waiting to prove that it can resist the attack of eyes even though dampened by real weather, even though historical atmosphere is mixed with exhaust like etymology with the use of a word or bone with sentence structure. No wonder we find it difficult to know our way about and tend to stay indoors.

This is not thinking, you said, more what colors it, like a smell entering our breath even to the seat of faith under the left nipple. Like the children I could have borne shaping my body toward submission and subterfuge. It is possible, I admitted, to do physics in inches as well as in centimeters, but a concept is more than a convenience. It takes us through earnest doorways to always the same kind of example. No chance of denser vegetation, of the cool shadow of firs extending this line of reasoning into the dark.

My love was deep and therefore lasted only the space of one second, unable to expand in more than one dimension at a time. The same way deeper meaning may constrict a sentence right out of the language into an uneasiness with lakes and ponds. In language nothing is hidden or our own, its light indifferent to holes in the present or postulates beginning with ourselves. Still, you may travel alone and yet be accompanied by my good wishes.

I wanted to settle down on a surface, a map perhaps, where my nearsightedness might help me see the facts. But grammar is deep. Even though it only describes, it submerges the mind in a maelstrom without discernable bottom, the dimensions of possibles swirling over the fixed edge of nothingness. Like looking into blue eyes all the way through to the blue sky without even a cloudbank or flock of birds to cling to. What are we searching behind the words as if a body of information could not also bruise? It is the skeleton that holds on longest to its native land.

Electric seasons. Night has become as improbable as a sea forever at high tide. The sheer excess of light makes for a lack of depth, denying our fall from grace, the way a membrane is all surface. Or the way we, clamoring for sense, exclude so many unions of words from the sphere of language. As if one could fall off the edge of the earth. Why do we fear the dark as unavoidable defeat when it alone is constant, and we'd starve if it stopped watering the lawn of dreams.

You were determined to get rid of your soul by expressing it completely, rubbing the silver off the mirror in hope of a new innocence of body on the other side of knowing. A limpid zone which would not wholly depend on our grammar in the way the sea draws its color from the sky. Noon light, harsh, without shadow. Each gesture intending only its involvement with gravity, a pure figure of reach, as the hyperbola is for its asymptotes or circles widening on the water for the stone that broke the surface. But the emigration is rallied, reflections regather across the ripples. Everything in our universe curves back to the apple.

As if I had to navigate both forward and backward, part of me turned away from where I'm going, taking the distance of long corridors to allow for delay and trouble, for keeping in the dark while being led on. In this way Chinese characters seem to offer their secret without revealing it, invitation to enter a labyrinth which, like that of the heart, may not have a center. It is replaced by being lost which I don't like to dwell on because the search for motivation can only drive us downward toward potential that is frightening in proportion to its depth and sluicegates to disappearance. It is much better, I have been advised, just to drift with the stream. The ink washes into a deeper language, and in the end the water runs clear.

Accelerating Frame

I badly wanted a story of my own. As if there were proof in spelling. But what if my experience were the kind of snow that does not accumulate? A piling of instants that did not amount to a dimension? What if wandering within my own limits I came back naked, with features too faint for the mirror, unequal to the demands of the night? In the long run I could not deceive appearances: Days and nights were added without adding up. Nothing to recount in bed before falling asleep. Even memory was not usable, a landscape hillocky with gravitation but without monuments, it did not hold the eye, did not hinder its glide toward the horizon where the prose of the world gives way to the smooth functioning of fear. If the wheel so barely touches the ground the speed must be enormous.

The concept of an inner picture is misleading. Like those on the screen, it takes the outer picture as a model, yet their uses are no more alike than statistics and bodies. Figures, we know, can proceed without any regard for reality, no matter how thin the fabric. True, the missing pieces can be glued in, but if you look for the deep you won't frighten your vertigo away. An ambition to fathom need not hold water. Stay on shore, put on more sweaters, and let the roar of the breakers swallow your urge to scream. If not the clouds themselves, their reflections withdraw with the tide. Then there is the familiar smell of wet sand and seaweed, debris of every kind, including hypodermics, condoms, oozing filth. My outer self comes running on pale legs to claim my share, while my inner picture stands dazed, blinking behind sunglasses, demanding a past that might redeem the present.

I knew that true or false is irrelevant in the pursuit of knowledge which must find its own ways to avoid falling as it moves toward horizons of light. We can't hope to prove gravity from the fact that it tallies with the fall of an apple when the nature of tallying is what Eve's bite called into question. My progress was slowed down by your hand brushing against my breast, just as travel along the optic nerve brakes the rush of light. But then light does not take place, not even in bed. It is like the kind of language that vanishes into communication, as you might into my desire for you. It takes attention focused on the fullness of shadow to give light a body that weighs on the horizon, though without denting its indifference.

I thought I could get to the bottom of things by taking my distance from logic, but only fell as far as the immediate. Here the moment flaunted its perfect roundness and could not be left behind because it accelerated with me, intense like roses blooming in the dark whereas I was still figuring out: are red roses at night darker than white ones, and all cats gray? But at some point we have to pass from explanation to description in the heroic hope that it will reach right out into experience, the groundswell flooding my whole being like heat or pollution, though the haze outside always looks as if it could easily be blown away. A cat of any color can descend into the pit behind her eyes and yawn herself right back to the bland surfaces that represent the world in the logical form we call reality. But logic is no help when you have no premises. And more and more people lacking the most modest form of them are wandering through the streets. Do we call the past perfect because it is out of sight? The present person singular is open to terrifying possibilities that strip off skin after skin · till I weep as when peeling onions.

The moments of intensity did not dazzle long. Even though they took my breath into a hollow empty of time, realm back behind thought, way back behind the ceiling I stared at as a child, it was a precarious shelter breeding its own rush back to the present that moves on whether all seats are taken or not. Only in time is there space for us, and crowded at that between antecedent and consequence, and narrow, narrow. I suddenly cried. The now cast its shadow over love. Sooner or later we look out of maternal mornings at the hard sun to check income and expenditure and find the operations covert, the deficit national. There are porters on the platform, pigeons preening in the breeze showing their glassy-eyed profile. Is this a description of what I saw, a quote, a proposition relevant as a lure for feeling, or a tangle of labels and wishes, with a blind spot reserved for the old woman with shopping bags due to walk through in a few minutes? I have no answer because seeing does not so much give precise reference as imply a motive, which is of no use, not even deductible when I assess the day gone by. But then it is already gone by.

It takes wrestling with my whole body for words on the tip of my tongue to be found later, disembodied, on paper. A paradox easily dissolved as any use of language is a passport to the fourth dimension, which allows us to predict our future, matter of body, even rock, thinning to a reflection that I hope outlasts both the supporting mirror and the slide from sign to scissors. Meanwhile, the crossing is difficult, maybe illegal, the documents doubtful, the road through darkness, wet leaves, rotting garbage, people huddling in doorways. The vehicle breaks down, the tenor into song. Again and again, the hand on paper as if tearing the tongue from its root, translating what takes place to what takes time. This, like any fission, may cause a burst of light. A body is consumed more quickly if the temperature accelerates into love. Art takes longer, as the proverb says, but likewise shortens life. We may also get stranded, caught on the barbed wire, muscles torn and useless for the speedway.

Finally I came to prefer the risk of falling to the arrogance of solid ground and placed myself on the thin line of translation, balancing precariously between body harnessed to slowness and categories of electric charge whizzing across fields nobody could stand on. Working the charge against my retina into the cognate red of a geranium I wondered if the direction of translation should be into arithmetic or back into my native silence. Or was this a question like right or left, reversible? And could it be resolved on the nonstandard model of androgyny, sharing out the sensitive zones among the contenders? Meanwhile everyday language is using all its vigor to keep the apple in the habit of falling though the curve of the world no longer fits our flat feet and matter's become too porous to place them on.

from A Key into the Language of America

Chapter I: Salutations

Are of two sorts and come immediately before the body. The pronunciation varies according to the point where the tongue makes contact with pumice found in great quantity. This lends credence, but no hand. Not so entirely Narragansett, the roof of the mouth. Position of hand or weapon conventional or volcanic formation.

Asco wequassunnúmmis. Good Morrow.
> sing
> salubrious
> imitation
> intimate

*I was born in a town on the other side which didn't want me in so many. All streets were long and led. In the center, a single person had no house or friends to **allay excessive sorrowe**. I, like other girls, forgot my name in the noise of traffic, opening my arms more to measure their extension than to offer embrace.*

> **the Courteous Pagan**
> barefoot and yes
> **his name laid down**
> **as dead**
> one openness
> one woman door
> so slow in otherwise
> so close

Chapter II: Of Eating and Entertainment

Indian corne, boiled with free will and predestination is a dish **exceeding wholesome** if taken through the mouth. Their words, too, fit to eat. And crow. A mark of "cadency." Similarly, an eye devouring its native region must devote special attention to its dialect. **Where they have themselves and their wives risen to prepare**. Against initiative of elements, against white bodies, against coining of new words: Tobacco. Unsuccessful.

> **Mishquockuk.**
> **Red Copper Kettle**.
> cycle
> chain
> for thought

I began my education by walking along the road in search of the heroic. I did not think to ask the way to the next well. Wilderness like fear a form of drunkenness or acting like a boy. The ground begins to slip. Rhythm of swallows seen from below. It is a strange truth that remains of contentment are yet another obstacle.

> the spelling in my mother's recipes
> explains
> why she gave birth to me
> and in the greatest heat should feed
> on me
> all flesh considered
> as a value

Chapter IV: Of Their Numbers

Without the help of Wall Street, how quick they are in casting up inalienable numbers. We do not have them. With help of hybrid corn instead of Europe's pens or poisons. Edge of ingenuity, between numb and nimble, forest or frigid wave before it crashes. Let it be considered whether a split providence or separate encystments in their own minds have taught them. Or concentration, its circular surface. What's called **arithmaticke**. A riddle on which matter rests.

Pawsuck. Of The Masculine Gender.
Pâwsuck. One Of The Feminine Gender.

Pâwsuck with time to dawdle, to cultivate lucidity and metric structure. Yet did not play by numbers. Too many messsengers that do not speak. A bowel movement every day and one war every generation. I feared becoming an object too boring for my bones to hold up, however clumsily.

> nostalgia figured
> in bruised shins
> and loss
> loss of eternity in triplicate
> such that my knees
> could come apart
> and tell
> their seeds

Chapter VII: Of Their Persons
and Parts of Body

Great bunch of **hayre** raked from darkness, yet as organized a physical substance as **sober English**. And can be photographed. In the brain, the proportion of quick apprehension to arable not less deep a structure than distinguished from limbs and labor or the central part of a document distinguished from title, nave, garment, soundbox or viscosity. Though childbirth will force christianity down the ladder into fighting units: women never forgive unparted flesh.

busy
guard
snatcher

I was shorn of illusion and impulse, though with a sorry knife, before touching amorous form. Where were my eyes? My heart was good and went to meet that difficult unfolding. Nudity in danger. All manner of man and of what bigness chased me to the bottom of my ignorance, desolately sublimating the fewness of wishes. Inexact report.

My long blue birth
snatched
from what sense of deed
what horizontal sleep whereas
a virgin marriageable
can slip
like fog in anywhere

Chapter X: Of the Season of the Yeere

They have thirteen moneths and are content to settle for that many. The courage to grow organs in reply to want, the way a giraffe stretches her neck to mounting advantage. If seasons can force the day around the sun there is no end to threshold or shedding skin. The chief difficulty with nature's outline yields hand-held exposures such as **Tashecautúmmo. How Many Years Since** fatal expression, since semantics, since influence.

able

ing

Made to sleep on the balcony, I tried to lord it over the kids still playing on the sidewalk. My space eked out by height, with family prejudice to back me up. With acute daring I dropped a tin box the way you drop a plumb-line down into sleep causing rings to widen out until a boy stuck his finger into the gob of spittle I had carefully placed inside. The shore fell into ruins.

machinery in place behind
hurt sharp
enough to trace
into the wiring of psychology
a risk of
membranes
undercuts the alibi

Chapter XII: Concerning the Heavens and Heavenly Lights

Which they adore, above acknowledging colonization. The stellar pallor attending powers shot madly from their spheres, the sky all over the earth, heaving its divine dimensions. If quickened circulation acts upon our thoughts, the moon so old it sets in full proportion. A light that does not slap you in the face, but raises nouns like navigation and transcendence. Nothing strange in pigment (black) that does not feed on side-stars obtained by imperfect combustion. Rocks. Meteorites. Great Western Railway.

> opalescent
> celestial
> celibacy

*An inner heat. an inflammation, predicting intimacies to hurt your eyes. Expanse of bodies, heavenly, observed **lying in the fields**. Frequent occasion. And measured by their angle **much observed in motion**, like the tin box tossed, sure curve belonging only to itself. Parabolas of the inanimate, these very children will throw stones.*

> toward sunset
> the uninvited guests
> have guns
> and written off
> red skin

> they (mis)
> take territory
> for imperative

Chapter XIII: Of the Weather

It may bee wondred why, New England being 12° neerer to the Sun, reality is yet in doubt. Some parts of winter act as lens owing to long reach as the **Nor West wind** comes under varying conditions and over loads of snow. If, when thin, the air unites the tribal factions, and a long vowel, more cold than overcast, **runnes about starke naked,** a climatic change occurs. American enough is all they know of atoms. Atmosphere windward like sexual feeling and as unpredictable, thick and vapory.

                    beaten
                    bound
                    cock
                    eye
                    under

My spittle overflowed literal expectations and was caught in flagrant light. Giggles sapped my resolve to leave home for unwobbling hyperbole. Inner darkness. Euphoric entropy. In a mixture of panic and mistaken gender I went West, intending the milky way. Common error.

                no one
                an island
                warmer than continents
                would
                in sharpest hemisphere
                would mobilize
                big masculine history
                on tap

Chapter XIV: Of the Winds

Accounts for eight cardinalls flying out of context though not explaining **the accurate division of the compasse** or where to blow. A motion that now buffets, now cools, has passed, more fertile in another period, the way tradition places God to **the Southwest of pleasingest** and passive.

What Think You When The Wind Blows From The East?

burn
fall
lass
rose
row
ow

The wind from a past only recently mine drove racial discrimination between the poles of my life and divided the city into usage and flooding. My family's limbs dispersed in reciprocities, but rejoined as if emerging out of water, more whole than before, but still bone-white as we lay on our bloated stomachs, as if already dead.

here
the wind
will be tomorrow
a constant disquisition
into the secret of
velocity
while men grow small
within their skin
tongue tied
into another language

Designed by
Samuel Retsov

Text: 10 pt Plantin

acid-free paper

Printed by
McNaughton & Gunn